PANDA
PARAMEDIC
AF268676

OPEN

Learn How To Help When
Peter Polar Bear's Heart Stops Beating

This is Panda Paramedic and her ambulance. She helps bears get to the hospital really quickly when they are super sick. Call her in an emergency!

Who is she going to help today...?

It's a lovely sunny day, and Peter Polar Bear is going to get his newspaper from Mr Sun Bear's shop.

"Good morning, I've your newspaper here," says Mr Sun Bear.

"Thanks," says Peter Polar Bear. "Can I sit on this chair and rest for a minute? I don't feel very well."

Suddenly, he wobbles and falls to the floor!

"Oh my goodness!" exclaims Mr Sun Bear.

Mr Sun Bear springs into action and checks for any **danger**. He takes hold of Peter Polar Bear by the shoulders and shakes him gently, trying to get a **response**, whilst shouting...

"Hello? Can you hear me? Open your eyes!"

Peter Polar Bear lies still on the floor; he doesn't wake up.

"Sonny, come quickly! Peter Polar Bear has **collapsed**. Dial **999**, we need Panda Paramedic. Once you have done that, please bring me the **defib**."

Sonny rushes to the phone
and dials **999**.

"We need Panda Paramedic
and the ambulance. Peter
Polar Bear has **collapsed**!"
he tells the call handler.

"We are at Sun Bear's Shop,"
he explains, when asked his
location. "Hurry, please!"

The call handler assures
him that Panda Paramedic
is on her way.

Mr Sun Bear tilts Peter Polar Bear's head back to open his airway and looks at his chest for up to ten seconds to check if he is breathing.

"Peter Polar Bear is not breathing. I need to start **CPR**" Says Mr Sun Bear.

Mr Sun Bear kneels at Peter Polar Bear's side and puts one paw on top of the other, pushing down hard and fast in the middle of his chest.

He does these pumps continuously and does not stop. Mr Sun Bear continues to do **paws-only CPR.**

Sonny runs through the door carrying a little machine, the **defib**!

"Great work, Sonny. Now, quickly, switch it on and follow the instructions."

The machine starts to speak. "Place pads on bear's chest, as shown in the picture," says the automated voice. Sonny looks at the picture on the pads and places the pads on Peter Polar Bear's chest just like the picture shows.

"Stand back! Analysing rhythm," the **defib** says. Mr Sun Bear stops giving **CPR**, and they both stand back...

"Shock advised! Check no one is touching the bear, then press the flashing button."

"Stand back! Shocking," Mr Sun Bear exclaims, then presses the button. Peter Polar Bear jolts, but doesn't wake up.

"Continue CPR," says the machine, and Mr Sun Bear does.

NEE NAR NEE NAR NEE NAR... here is Panda Paramedic with her ambulance. "Hello, I'm Panda Paramedic and I'm here to help. What has happened?"

"Peter Polar Bear has suddenly **collapsed**. He didn't wake up when I called to him, and he wasn't breathing, so we've started **CPR**. He's had one shock from the **defib**," Sonny replies.

"Excellent job, bears! Well done, using your lifesaving **CPR** skills," says Panda Paramedic. "I'll take it from here."

The **defib** interrupts, "Stand back! Analysing rhythm".

Mr Sun Bear stops giving **CPR,** and they all listen.

"Shock advised. Press flashing button."

Panda paramedic checks no-one is touching Peter Polar Bear.

"Stand back! Shocking," she says, and presses the button.

Again Peter Polar Bear jolts, but does not wake up.

Panda Paramedic takes over giving **CPR.**

"Grrrr, uhhh, grrrr," groans Peter Polar Bear.

"Did you hear that, bears? That is a **sign of life**. I need to check him over," exclaims Panda Paramedic, shaking his shoulders.

"Peter Polar Bear, can you hear me? Open your eyes."

"GRRR, UHHH, GRRR," groans Peter Polar Bear more loudly.

Panda Paramedic continues to assess Peter Polar Bear.

"Peter Polar Bear is breathing, and his heart is now beating again, but he is not fully awake. We must take him to the hospital. He's still really sick. Can you please bring the stretcher from the ambulance?"

Sonny and Mr Sun Bear hurry to the ambulance and bring the stretcher. Peter Polar Bear is loaded carefully onto it.

"WAIT..." Sonny shouts. He runs to the counter to retrieve Peter Polar Bear's newspaper and places it on his lap. "You nearly forgot this!"

The stretcher is loaded into the ambulance with Peter Polar Bear safely fastened in. Panda Paramedic drives to the hospital.

NEE NAR NEE NAR the sirens blare. She arrives at the hospital in super quick time.

"Hello, Nurse Moon Bear and Doctor Moon Bear. Peter Polar Bear has had a sudden **cardiac arrest**. He's had CPR and two shocks from the defib; then he started breathing, and his heart started beating. He is not fully awake and is still really sick."

"Thank you for taking such good care of him. We will run some tests, give him some medicine, and continue to look after him," says Doctor Moon Bear.

Peter Polar Bear is soon feeling well again thanks to the help given to him by all the bears in Bear Town. And he even gets to read his newspaper!

Glossary

danger - when helping someone you must always make sure that you are safe and not placed in danger.

collapsed - has fallen down and will not wake up. There is no **response** when you shout and shake them gently.

999 - emergency telephone number to ring the emergency services. You can contact the police, ambulance service, fire brigade or coastguard using this number.

defib / defibrillator - a machine that can give an electric shock to the heart of someone who is in cardiac arrest.

cpr / cardiopulmonary resuscitation - a lifesaving skill that can help a person to stay alive when they have stopped breathing and the heart has stopped beating. Consists of chest compressions and, if trained to do so, mouth-to-mouth / rescue breaths.

pumps / chest compressions - pushing down hard and fast in the centre of a person's chest to pump the heart.

paws-only CPR / hands-only CPR - uninterrupted chest compressions at a rate of 2 compressions per second.

pads - the defib has sticky pads that stick on a person's chest. They stick under the right collar bone and left armpit.

sign of life - the person has started to move, breathe and groan. This may mean the heart has restarted.

cardiac arrest - when the heart stops beating and pumping blood, and the person becomes unresponsive.

Fill In The Blanks

Check for **D**___________ to make sure you are safe.

Try to get a **R**___________ by shouting and shaking them gently.

S_______ for help and dial 999.

Open the **A**_________ by tilting the head back so they can breathe.

Check for **B**_______________ ,If not breathing...

start **C**___

Use a **D**________ if one is available.

Go to www.pandaparamedic.com to check out the answers

Can you spot 5 differences?

Can you find the words?

R	C	I	D	E	M	A	R	A	P	I	S	S	H
D	D	E	F	I	B	R	I	L	L	A	T	O	R
O	L	A	A	I	R	W	A	Y	D	M	U	S	E
E	C	N	B	O	H	E	E	D	A	S	C	S	P
P	O	E	R	P	M	P	A	C	O	L	S	P	A
S	L	W	E	E	R	P	T	S	I	R	A	L	R
T	L	S	A	C	R	A	P	A	P	B	R	L	E
R	A	P	T	N	F	D	N	A	A	U	O	A	T
E	P	A	H	A	N	S	U	R	N	B	M	P	E
T	S	P	I	L	S	N	E	P	O	D	E	P	O
C	E	E	N	U	C	D	R	H	A	D	A	E	S
H	D	R	G	B	R	E	M	L	P	H	I	N	E
E	F	I	T	M	R	C	O	M	R	T	R	T	R
R	N	T	R	A	H	R	G	N	P	U	F	F	S

DEFIBRILLATOR
PANDA
AMBULANCE
STRETCHER
OPEN
PUMPS
PARAMEDIC
BREATHING
CPR
NEWSPAPER
AIRWAY
PADS
COLLAPSED
PUFFS

Can you colour me in?

CERTIFICATE

OF COMPLETION

THIS IS TO CERTIFY THAT

----

has succesfully learnt how to help a person
when the heart has stopped beating

PANDA
PARAMEDIC

BOOK ONE

OPEN

PANDA
PARAMEDIC